T0374311

Between the Lines

Sandeep Kaur and Varsha Venkatakrishna

Order this book online at www.trafford.com
or email orders@trafford.com

Most Trafford titles are also available at major online book retailers.

Printed in the United States of America.

ISBN: 978-1-4269-9292-6 (sc)
ISBN: 978-1-4269-9293-3 (e)

Library of Congress Control Number: 2011914974

Trafford rev. 10/19/2011

 www.trafford.com

North America & international
toll-free: 1 888 232 4444 (USA & Canada)
phone: 250 383 6864 ♦ fax: 812 355 4082

Contents

Haikus

Tankas

Life to Death

What is Life?
A sequence of events over time?
Or a book with no rhyme?

What is Life?
Is it a never ending hole in which you fall?
Or is it a heaven open to all?

What is Life?
Is it merely just the opposite of death?
Or is it the thing that keeps my blood running fresh?

If all these words don't correctly define,
Then what is their truth for which they are divine?

Keeping in mind all the given virtues
I have come to one single, lone truth.

Life merely is not just a toy,
Not something with which to ploy.

Life is something valuable and sincere.
Just comprehending this will make everything clear.

So, please, listen to me once, my friend,
Hear my heart and try to understand.

I have lived, therefore, I know.
Life can conceal, and it can be put as show.

I say, treat it with care,
Give it its share.
Who knows what might not be there?

I say, live for the living,
Gift to the gifting,
And bow to the bowing.

At one time, life will come so near
That death will be very clear.

But until that time comes,
Live life as though it just begun.

Life is a gift, not a toy.
Live life with care but with much joy.

By: Sandeep Kaur

Soulful Freedom

I run free with the air
I soar above the skies everywhere

I count the stars in the realm of night
I embrace them in my arms, so tight

I lead the birds through the mysterious skies
Filled with freedom, in the heavens they fly.

Catching every raindrop escaping the waterfall,
I hear the voices above me call

Unresting, they try to lure me in
To sit upon the heavens along with them

Without the liberty of choice
I follow my heart's own voice

As I eagerly drift far, far above
My eyes brighten with lights of love

Being pulled beyond reality,
I drift to a world of mystery

Finally calming down with a sigh,
I find myself with nowhere to pry

Surrounded by a unique type of bright
Filled everywhere with luminescent light,

A restfulness fills my core
Leaving me with breaths no more

I lie down to rest in peace
My existence beginning to cease.

By: Sandeep Kaur

Love doesn't end with Eternity

The sun arises with a new day,
each ray embracing the world,
each twinkle kissing flower petals.

You arise to greet the morning,
only then is it complete,
complete with your beauty.

Nature's musicians hush with your passing
momentarily taken aback by the possibility
that such a creation were possible.

The dew twinkles as it meets the sun
yet falls dull suddenly
looking at the twinkle in your eye.

But, the most sacred of all are those roses
lucky enough to be touched willingly
brushing against your delicate visage.

Life's twists and turns
with lackluster nights and days
beckon a simple ray of light.

A ray that adds meaning,
a light that frightens darkness away,
a love that doesn't end with eternity.

By:Sandeep Kaur

By My Side

What does it mean
to have you by my side?

Does it mean the sun
will rise in the east
and set in the west, dragging
the light up and across
the ocean while leaving
behind jewels as it
descends to rest and
gather energy for another
round the next day?

Does it mean the ground
will grow and die while
in its youth, sprouting
colors across lands and
darkening them in middle age
with reds, browns, and oranges,
flying through the years
as the colors dissolve to
complete white while dying?

Does it mean the clouds
will weep till they can weep
no more, pouring out their
grief while moistening the
life over which they
prevail day after day as
they travel land after land
like ants in search of food,
crawling about helplessly?

Or does it mean you,
you will be by my side
every moment that sun
awakens and goes to sleep,
every time the colors of
the land morph into each
other, every wind felt by
the weeping clouds, you,
you will be by my side?

By: Sandeep Kaur

We are One

They say,
you and I are
two distant stars.

What truth do their
words hold?

They say,
He is with those
who open their hearts.

What honesty was hidden
within belief?

They spoke
as the world commanded,
uplifting minds, barren souls.

But, my love,
you and I are
the one twinkling star.

Lights amidst
the vastly demeaning darkness
calming those frightened below

We, my love,
leaves of one tree,
sprout, breathe, fall once.

By: Sandeep Kaur

A Questioning Proposal

Wilst thou grant the greatest
gift one may bestow upon another,
the treasured sympathy said
to protrude of one's bosom?

Wilst thou depart of thy mind
any implacable deductions
as to taint my nature thereof
to subside alongside solitude?

For, the lovingly merry breeze
shall once again weave
our tale of life, of love,
no longer strayed by hills.

For, pastures shall bloom once more
beautifying the earth around
and we shall often visit
the birthplace of our love.

Wilst thou agree upon my company
to complete thine days hereafter,
to stir life in thine dreams,
to place happiness at thine feet?

For, barren of thy presence am I,
drowning in a sea of solitude.
Wilst thou lend me thy hand,
grant me the boon of beatitude?

By: Sandeep Kaur

A Valediction: of what is dearest to me

Ah, what grace,
my dear,
the sun hath,
showered o'er thee.
What ostentatious gleam,
my dear,
hath it bathed thee.
Ah, what music,
my dear,
the breeze weaves.
What a rhythm,
my dear,
it strums in thee.

If only,
my dear,
the Lord hath given
the land equality.
If only,
my dear,
it had thy beauty,
thy colors,
my dear,
would it be complete.

If only,
my dear,
the Lord hath given
the rain equality.
If only,
my dear,
hath it consolidated
the thirstful animals
the manner thy comfort,
my dear,
hath reached me.

Such a similarity,
my dear,
may never be.
Simple it is not,
my dear,
to mirror such beauty,
such grace, and
spreading of tranquility
as bestowed upon
my dear.

By: Sandeep Kaur

Foolish Mind!

Great philosophers pronounce one subject
　　　　　one subject in numerous texts,
yet in You there comes no sense,
　　　　　You comprehend the rest.

A single reason before Your eyes,
　　　　　yet You search about,
A single reason, one Truth,
　　　　　yet You bloom in doubt!

Comprehend You not the facts true,
　　　　　what is the eternal truth.
You search about for the lost joy
　　　　　that before You takes root.

Why question the wondrous eternal being,
　　　　　the one who created You,
Decorated You, gifted You feelings,
　　　　　placed His light in You?

Without His existence, exists none
　　　　　even blackness escapes.
How will You thrive without the light,
　　　　　what will You make?

In all the places You look about,
　　　　　in all is His presence.
In all the beings, monuments here
　　　　　in all the divine essence.

Open your shutters, You Foolish Mind,
      look outside Your cage.
Look at what the foreground presents,
      see Your part in His game.

Peace does not prevail where
      suffering is contented.
Suffering is forever present
      as long as You are blinded.

All You take in of the world
      is only but illusion,
Ground, Earth, planets, universe,
      none here as permanent.

Soon the End will be near,
      only One will remain.
Be afraid, show some fear,
      correct Your wrong-doings.

Tarry not till it is too late
      now is the time to awaken.
Beware! The End will be great,
      all will be forsaken.

Repent now, or You'll repent later
      allow no sins evermore.
Fold Your hands before the Giver,
      cleanse the filth in Your core!

By: Sandeep Kaur

A Face

Mirror, mirror on the wall
who is that you show?
A familiar face
yet not familiar at all.

The irises deep as the sky
seen at midnight
with a miniscule shine,
depth with nowhere to pry.

The nose fixed in place
high in the air
determined with passion
part of that face.

The skin stretched tight
with youth at its peak,
a golden gleam,
a tint dark yet bright.

The mouth, a curvy shape
flowing from cheek to cheek,
ripples like liquid,
not effortless to recreate.

Mirror, mirror on the wall,
the face you show
is familiar indeed,
familiar, yet not at all.

By: Sandeep Kaur

I am Here

As drowning silk, this time flows
Blue, light blue this silence.

Nowhere is the ground
Nowhere the sky.

The lonely breeze whispers
Only you are here.

There is only me, my breaths, my heartbeats
Such depths, such loneliness.

And me, only me.
I believe in my existence, my presence.

By: Sandeep Kaur

A Secret

There is a secret that has not approached lips.
It only creeps in the eyes.

At times, from you, at times, from me
it pleads for some words.

Whomever it adores the lips of,
it wraps arms around that voice.

But, what this secret is,
it is a feeling, a whole feeling.

A scent there is
as if swimming in the wind.

A billowing scent
that lacks but a voice,

Whose location you also realize,
whose presence I am also aware of.

Even from the world, it does not hide.
What type of secret is this?

By: Sandeep Kaur

Consolidations

Whenever the cloud of pain hovered,
Whenever the shadow of sorrow moved,
When the tears inside brimmed over,
When this lonely heart in fear did cover,
I consolidated that heart with words as such:

Oh, Heart! At last, why do you weep?
This is how all happens in the world.
These deep emotions, delicate bonds,
Time has donated to all.
A little sorrow is everyone's share.
A little sunshine is everyone's share.
Every moment is a new season.
Why do you lose such moments?
At last, Heart, why do you weep?

Consolidations in the form of words,
Words as such reached out
Only to halt at touching my heart.

By: Sandeep Kaur

There was a Time

Since the time
your eyes touched mine,
spreading a feeling: sublime

Since the time
my ears, your voice did hear,
replacing passion in place of fear

Since the time
your scent embraced me,
killing any hope of sanity

Since the time
your touch burned my skin,
cleansing my heart, my veins within

Since that time,
I know no other
from whom I need not cover

Since that time
nowhere is there a place
where your presence has no trace

Since that time
I have become aware
never is there a moment to spare

Since that time
the wind seems more free,
Love, with open arms, embraces me.

By: Sandeep Kaur

Remember Me

Remember me when the years have passed,
When wretched aging has taken course
Oh how on rocky banks we'd danced
Until our calloused feet were sore.
Laughing in the garden's perfume,
Far away from the bronzed sun.
While admiring the moon kissed tulips bloom,
The quiet calling of the clocks were shunned.
And now, as my ancient flesh decays,
Withering into the unknown abyss
I vow to never forget the days,
Of which I cannot help but reminisce.
Please, forget me not when I have passed,
he earthly flesh our memories will outlast.

By: Varsha Venkatakrishna

The Rose

In my garden is a flower more beautiful than the rest,
So delicate and fine that every being it lures;
A simple rose of scarlet red, it is so fine and beautifully demure,
That all creatures visit it, from bees in hives and birds in nests.
Soft rain on its velvety surface do press,
Forming round spheres that glimmer when matured,
And such splendor cannot be harmed by silly pests.
But what if this rose would wilt?
All its wonders will be gone in a moment;
Its petals will die, those that were smoother than silk.
More sorrow I think I have not felt
For my lovely, dear tender flower,
Of which I love much more than myself.

By: Varsha Venkatakrishna

A Poem

What's a poem but mastery of sense,
Of complex grammar wrought with greatest care,
Of meters, lines, and glistening ornaments.
Steered by winds of wise that to none compare.
A dress of silk so greatly sewn it seems
So seamless, by every tailor its sought;
So perfect that it flows in glossy streams
And sings much softer than a cradle rocks.
From where does it come? This good, loving hand
though sometimes amateur, forever deft
Each syllable and tiny turn is planned
'Till words do disappear and art is left.
It touches lands that kiss mighty seas --
A poem is beauty, and all of these.

By: Varsha Venkatakrishna

Night Skies

The harmonized rhythm of the night
Descends from mist as the trees turn to it\
The cicada's hum and speeding trains
Slash through the eternal quiet.
Crushed by selfish agendas,
While walking in the simplest gait
Not entirely paying attention
At the tears that have already dried.
Part the clouds with your cobalt gazes
And repaint the sky
Cold hair clings to wet fingers,
Unhappy to say goodbye.

By: Varsha Venkatakrishna

Thoughts at Night

Looking at the sky that is jeweled with the moon
And freckled with stars that hold my destiny,
I wonder what it will take to reach the sky.

Tonight I wish to leave the weary heat of June,
Leap, and fly to the cunning twins of Gemini,
and laugh at the chained unfortunates I pass by.

But what if I am suddenly flung to Earth,
or burnt when I finally touch the stars,
and forced to taste the bitter tangs of failure?

As I contemplate, my confidence fades into dearth
and I am returned to the mundane sound of rushing cars
I decide for or now I will stay on the ground, far from possible
danger.

By: Varsha Venkatakrishna

In 5 Minutes

In a minute, my heart went numb
From naïveness crushed by truth
And into darkness, my soul succumbed,
Weak within its youth.
Within 9 seconds, my eyes turned red
Where teardrops always clung
As I lay within my night-chilled bed,
My lullaby left unsung.

By: Varsha Venkatakrishna

Good Poetry

I hate the rules
and regulations of poetry
Clauses, meters, and lines
do not make good poems.
Rather, it's the
willingness of the writer
to open his heart
and write his mind.
Only then can
there truly be
good poetry.

By: Varsha Venkatakrishna

The Garden Room

Beyond the ivory bedroom,
Past the golden vase,
If you brush back the violet curtains,
You will come face-to-face

With a brown oak door,
Smartly hidden from view,
Found by only those who know it,
and used by a privileged few.

Twist open the handle,
And slowly step inside,
Into a world of my creation -
The source of my joy and pride.

Inside you will find a garden,
Concealed from public's sight,
Once within, it's easy to find,
Nature's true wondrous might.

Past the threshold the magic begins,
As one sees the flowers bloom,
Deep inside, fires burns bright,
When inside my Garden Room.

By: VarshaVenkatakrishna

It Still Remains

Like an echo, where
Whispers can be heard
Even after the voices have left,

Like the rain, where
Droplets still sprinkle
Even after the showers have passed,

You still hurt me so
Even after all these years.

By: VarshaVenkatakrishna

Haikus

Soft Snow Swirling

Soft snow swirling
Outside, a small brown doe stares
At the breaking dawn.

By: Varsha Venkatakrishna

Ticking Away

I'm ticking away
the minutes of lost moments
that we could have shared

By: Varsha Venkatakrishna

Bella Luce

Bella Luce (noun):
the sight of endless wonder,
a beautiful light.

By: Varsha Venkatakrishna

Over

It's all said and done
The sadness is behind me
And I don't turn back.

By: Varsha Venkatakrishna

Birds

Turquoise speckled eggs,
cardinals, pregnant with song,
the voices of spring.

By: Varsha Venkatakrishna

The Truth

Spending time with you
Quite frankly speaking, my dear,
Is like eating fire.

By: Varsha Venkatakrishna

Paradise

Shallow shores shimmer
Soft sounds from salient streams
Cooling, calming coves.

By: Varsha Venkatakrishna

Caught

Caught in the middle
of two worlds, each trying to
quickly reel me in.

By: Varsha Venkatakrishna

Life of a Dancer

First, a harsh warm-up
then, dance 'till your body's sore
just an average day

By: Varsha Venkatakrishna

Trampoline

The springs stretch with stress
as the jumpers gleefully play
in the humid air.

By: Varsha Venkatakrishna

Morning Times

I don't brush away
the frost that lines the windows
in the morning light.

By: Varsha Venkatakrishna

Lake of Harmony

Lake of Harmony
splishing, splashing at our feet,
our calming sea.

By: Sandeep Kaur

A Sunset

Sunset, sea of love
smiling so brightly on all,
you bid us goodnight.

By: Sandeep Kaur

Sunflower's leaf

Growing with much speed
Oh, sunflower's great green leaf!
Drink all the sunshine

By: Sandeep Kaur

Tankas

A Rage

Rage, beyond anger
Fire licking at my heart
Flames burying all
Sweetly suppressing sorrow
Taking me down with warm arms

By: Sandeep Kaur

Great Joy

Wild joy with no words
Like butterflies with no wings
Spreads like fireworks
Ends with magnificent speed
Leaving a desert behind.

By: Sandeep Kaur

Confusion

Turns of confusion
Winds whirling around with rage
Twisting and turning
Answers giving them a stop
Gifting all questions with a break.

By: Sandeep Kaur

Memories

Long lost memories
That past life that once was mine
Hidden now, unseen
Has left cherished dreams behind
Taking with it heart, soul, and mind

By: Sandeep Kaur

A New Day Arouses

Such a day has come
Of the color of your cheeks
Life has just begun
A bright joy, scent, love so sweet
This feeling, I wish to keep.

By: Sandeep Kaur

The Thing Called Life

As the time passes
So does pass the thing called life
Many in great masses
Happily, with no great plight
Leave with joy the thing called life.

By: Sandeep Kaur

In My Times

There have passed many days
When my sun rose in the west
I wrestled my way
To pass those difficult tests,
Emerge in life at my best.

By: Sandeep Kaur

Beauty

A face of beauty
Speaks nothing of what's inside
Who needs such beauty
Whose company quickly dies?
True beauty's home is inside.

By: Sandeep Kaur